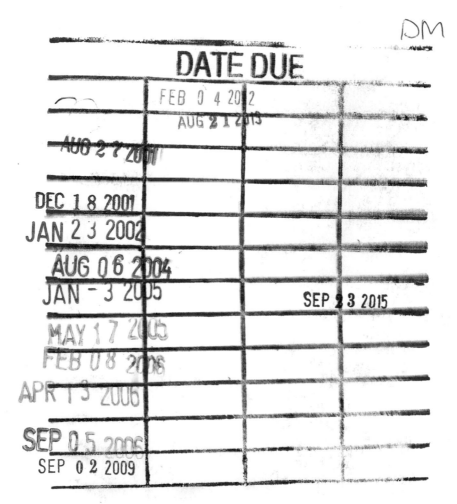

# ENDANGERED!

**TIGERS**

## Amanda Harman

Series Consultant: James G. Doherty
General Curator, The Bronx Zoo, New York

## BENCHMARK BOOKS

MARSHALL CAVENDISH
NEW YORK

Benchmark Books
Marshall Cavendish Corporation
99 White Plains Road
Tarrytown, New York 10591-9001

Library of Congress Cataloging-in-Publication Data

Harman, Amanda.
    Tigers / Amanda Harman.
        p.    cm. — (Endangered!)
    Includes index.
    Summary: Describes the physical characteristics, habitat, and
behaviors of this largest cat in the world which is in danger of
dying out because of hunting and destruction of its forest home.
    ISBN 0-7614-0215-2 ( lib. bdg. )
    1.  Tigers—Juvenile literature.    2.  Endangered species—Juvenile
literature.    [ 1. Tigers.  2.  Endangered species. ]    I. Title.
II. Series.
QL737.C23H35  1996
599.74'428—dc20                                           95-19294
                                                               CIP
                                                               AC


Printed in Hong Kong

**PICTURE CREDITS**
*The publishers would like to thank the Frank Lane Picture Agency (FLPA) for
supplying all the photographs used in this book except for the following:* 11, 27
Silvestris (via FLPA); 14 Sunset (via FLPA); 22 The Tiger Trust.

Series created by Brown Packaging

Front cover: Indian tiger.
Title page: Female Indian tiger with cub.
Back cover: Indian tiger.

# Contents

*A male tiger shows off his fearsome teeth.*

# Introduction

Tigers are the largest cats in the world. They are cousins of lions and leopards and of our pet cats. The tiger is easy to recognize. It usually has a thick, reddish gold coat, with black or gray stripes over its body and black-and-white patterns on its face.

A tiger's body is strong and powerful. Its huge paws have sharp, curved claws. When the tiger roars, it opens its mouth wide, showing its long **canine teeth**. Tigers are beautiful animals, but they are also ferocious hunters. People both love and fear them.

There have been cats on Earth for millions of years. During that time some kinds have disappeared. These cats could not **adapt** to natural changes that took place, and they became **extinct**. Today, tigers are in danger of dying out, not for natural reasons but because people hunt them and destroy their forest homes. Once, over 100,000 tigers lived in the wild. Now there are only about 7000 left at the most. If something is not done to save these wonderful animals soon, they may vanish forever.

*An Indian tiger watches from a leafy perch. This is an unusual picture, since tigers do not often climb trees.*

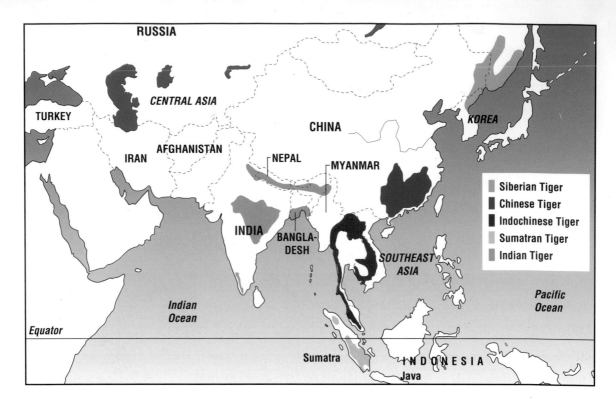

RUSSIA

CENTRAL ASIA

TURKEY

IRAN

AFGHANISTAN

NEPAL

MYANMAR

CHINA

KOREA

INDIA

BANGLA-
DESH

SOUTHEAST
ASIA

Indian
Ocean

Pacific
Ocean

Equator

Sumatra

INDONESIA
Java

| | Siberian Tiger |
| | Chinese Tiger |
| | Indochinese Tiger |
| | Sumatran Tiger |
| | Indian Tiger |

# Where Tigers Live

There is only one kind of tiger. However, tigers are known by different names depending on the general area in which they live. Those from the Russian region of Siberia and from Korea and northern China are known as Siberian tigers, while those that live in southeastern China are called Chinese tigers. Indochinese tigers come from Southeast Asia, and Indian tigers from India, Nepal, Bangladesh, and northern Myanmar (formerly Burma). Sumatran tigers live only on the Indonesian island of Sumatra.

All tigers live in pretty much the same way and face similar problems. Tigers from different areas differ from one another in size, color, and markings.

*Areas where tigers can be found*

The biggest tigers are the Siberian tigers. An adult male can measure up to 13 ft (4 m) long from its head to the tip of its tail and weigh as much as 570 lb (260 kg). Females are a little smaller. Sumatran tigers are the smallest. A male Sumatran tiger measures up to 9 ft (2.7 m) in length and can weigh up to 380 lb (150 kg). Sumatran tigers also look the most stripy, since their stripes are the closest together.

Chinese tigers are the least stripy tigers and also the least plentiful. Only 30-80 survive in the wild. Indian tigers are the most numerous, with possibly 4700 living in the wild. Indian tigers usually have the reddish gold fur and black stripes that are common for tigers. On rare occasions, Indian tigers are born with pure white fur and black stripes.

*Besides having different colored fur than other tigers, white Indian tigers have different colored eyes. They are blue instead of the usual brown.*

## Where Tigers Live

Tigers used to be found throughout mainland Asia and on the islands of Bali, Java, and Sumatra in Indonesia. Now tigers have disappeared from many parts of this **range**. The Bali tiger became extinct in 1950. The Caspian tiger, which used to live in Afghanistan, Iran, Turkey, and parts of Central Asia, died out in 1965. There was also the Javan tiger. Some people say they still see Javan tigers, but scientists think that the last one died in 1979.

Tigers can be found in a number of different **habitats**. Many tigers live in forests, including **tropical rainforests**, mountain forests, and snow-covered northern forests. Some also live in dry grasslands, while others live in marshy swamps. Tigers' markings allow them to remain well hidden. Their reddish gold fur and dark stripes mingle with

*The tiger's striped coat usually looks very striking. But a tiger hiding in long grass can be difficult to see!*

the shadows and patches of sunlight caused by tall grasses and trees. Their paws are soft and padded so they can move silently through the undergrowth.

The Siberian tiger lives in areas where the ground is covered by snow during the long winter months. Here the temperature may drop as low as -49 degrees Fahrenheit (-45 degrees Celsius). However, this tiger is particularly well adapted to cold conditions. It has a layer of fat underneath an extra-thick coat to keep it warm. Sometimes this fat layer can be 2 in (5 cm) thick. The Siberian tiger's coat is lighter in color than those of other kinds of tigers. In the winter it gets even lighter, so that the tiger stands out as little as possible when hunting in snowy northern forests.

*A Siberian tiger pictured in the snowy wastes of southeastern Russia. A tiger remains alert at all times – even when it stops to take a drink.*

9

*A tiger must keep a close eye on the boundaries of its territory, as this Sumatran tiger is doing, otherwise a neighboring tiger may move in.*

# Claiming Territories

Adult tigers usually spend much of their time alone. Each tiger has its own area of land called a **territory**. The tiger spends all its time here, hunting, eating and drinking, or resting. A study in Nepal found that a female tiger's territory may cover about 8 square miles (20 square km). A male's may cover 23-40 square miles (60-105 square km) because males are bigger and need more prey.

To make sure that other tigers keep away, tigers spend a lot of their time patrolling their boundaries and leaving "signposts" that say whose territory it is. These signposts may be made by scratching the bark on tree trunks or by scent marking. To leave scent marks, tigers rub their faces against the tree trunks or spray their urine on trees, bushes, grasses, and rocks. Tigers roar, too, to warn others to keep out of their territory – at night, a tiger's roar can sometimes be heard over 7½ miles (12 km) away!

Sometimes, though, a tiger does ignore the scent markings and enters another's territory. If the owner of the territory discovers the intruder, the two cats will fight until one of them runs away or is killed.

*Two Indian tigers fighting. Tigers do not like to fight. Even if they are not killed they may be injured, and a bad injury can stop a tiger from hunting. If it cannot hunt, it may starve.*

# On the Prowl

Tigers are **carnivores**. They eat many small animals, such as insects, birds, and monkeys. But their favorite foods are large, hoofed **mammals**, such as wild pigs, deer, antelopes, and buffaloes. Sometimes they even attack young elephants or rhinoceroses.

Tigers are so strong they can pull down and kill animals up to four times their own size. This is just as well, because tigers may eat up to about 40 lb (18 kg) of meat a day for a few days in a row. Tigers catch animals by creeping up on

*An Indian tiger hunting. A tiger can travel 12 miles (19 km) in one night in search of food.*

them quietly and then dashing out at them. A tiger relies on its hearing and excellent sight when it hunts. At night, a tiger can see more than five times as well as a person can.

Once it has spotted its **prey**, the tiger crouches down low with its head up and moves silently through the undergrowth with slow and careful footsteps. Every once in a while, it stops for a moment, before continuing quietly. When it is about 60 ft (18 m) away from its target, the tiger stops once more, waits, and then rushes forward to attack.

*Animals like this swamp deer must always be on the lookout for tigers. Tigers attack suddenly, and deer need all the warning they can get.*

The tiger has two methods of catching its unlucky victim. It may knock it off its feet with one of its huge forepaws and then pounce on it, or it may be able to seize the animal right away, usually by the throat or back of the neck. A tiger's forelegs and massive shoulders have large muscles. These give it the power to grab and hold on to its prey while its back feet stay firmly on the ground. The tiger uses its long, sharp claws to grip the struggling animal. Like those of a pet cat, these claws are usually held in slots in the tiger's paws when the animal is not hunting.

Tigers sometimes kill their prey with a neck-breaking bite to the back of its neck. Often, though, a tiger will

*The tiger's hind legs are longer than its forelegs. This allows the animal to spring forward in a leap of up to 38 ft (11 m).*

clamp its jaws around the animal's throat and squeeze. This prevents the victim from breathing, and it soon dies.

Deer and antelope can flee very quickly. Tigers do not often catch these animals in a chase, and so do not waste their energy. If the tiger misses the animal on its first pounce, it will normally chase it for no more than 220 yards (200 m). Despite being skillful hunters, tigers catch only one out of every ten animals that they target.

Even when tigers do bring down an animal, sometimes they lose it to another hunter. In some parts of Asia, there

*This Indian tiger has just killed a hog deer by squeezing the animal's throat so that it could not breathe.*

is a type of wild dog called the dhole, which hunts the same animals as the tiger does. Although dholes are much smaller than tigers, these dogs live and hunt in large groups. If a tiger and a group of dhole come into contact over an animal the tiger has killed, the dholes do not hesitate to chase the tiger off.

*The dhole can eat over 8 lb (4 kg) of meat in an hour. This Asian wild dog is one of the tiger's few enemies – but only when it is part of a group. Like the tiger, though, the dhole is in danger of becoming extinct.*

After a successful hunt, a tiger drags its prey to the nearest bush or patch of long grass. It then begins to feed. All the time it is eating, the tiger growls and snarls loudly to warn any other animals to keep away. If the animal it has caught is large, the tiger may leave it from time to time and return when it is hungry again. Within about three days there is nothing left of the prey but skin and bone.

Tigers are active mainly when it is cool – in the evening, at night, and in the early morning. During the heat of the day, they usually find a shady spot to lie in or they may spend hours in a pool of water.

*A tiger pulls its kill out of sight, while another tiger looks on. It is unusual to see two adult tigers together. These two are probably a breeding male and female.*

# Raising Young

Tigers **mate** for the first time when they are three to four years old. Usually males mate with as many females as possible. Mating may take place at any time of the year. It is most likely to happen between November and April in the northern part of the tiger's range.

The males can tell when it is time to mate because the females release a special scent that indicates that they are ready. However, the breeding season is usually the only time when adult male tigers and adult females get together. Therefore, before mating takes place, the pair take some time to get to know each other.

*This Indian tiger cub is about two weeks old. Its eyes have probably just opened for the first time.*

Between three and four months after mating, females give birth to babies called cubs. There may be one to six cubs, but usually there are two or three. The cubs are tiny when they are born, weighing about 2 lb (1 kg) each. They are blind and totally helpless. By now, the father has disappeared, and the mother has to bring up her cubs alone.

For the first four to eight weeks of their life, the cubs are hidden away in a special hiding place called a **den**. This might be in a cave, a hollow tree, or among some thick bushes or tall grasses. Here they are protected from animals that would eat them if they found them, such as hyenas, leopards, and jackals.

*By the age of six months, a tiger cub is quite large – and can be quite a handful!*

During this time, the mother goes out on short hunting trips every five to six days. But she cannot go too far, because, like other mammals, she has to feed the cubs regularly with her milk. The cubs continue to receive their mother's milk until they are about five months old, even though they start eating meat at about six weeks of age.

The cubs go hunting with their mother from the age of about six months. At first they hide in the bushes and watch what she does to learn the correct way to catch their

*An Indian tigress and her two cubs feed from a kill that she has made.*

prey. Then they practice on small animals and birds such as peacocks, or by playfighting with one another. When they are about two or two and a half years old, the cubs leave their mother. They set up their own territories and have to learn to survive on their own.

Only about half the tiger cubs born survive for more than two years, and many die very young. In the wild, the lucky ones live for about 15 years, while tigers in **captivity** may live for 20 years. The oldest tiger ever known lived until it was 26 years old.

*In this picture, one cub has the other playfully by the throat. But in later life, the tiger will use this grip to kill its prey.*

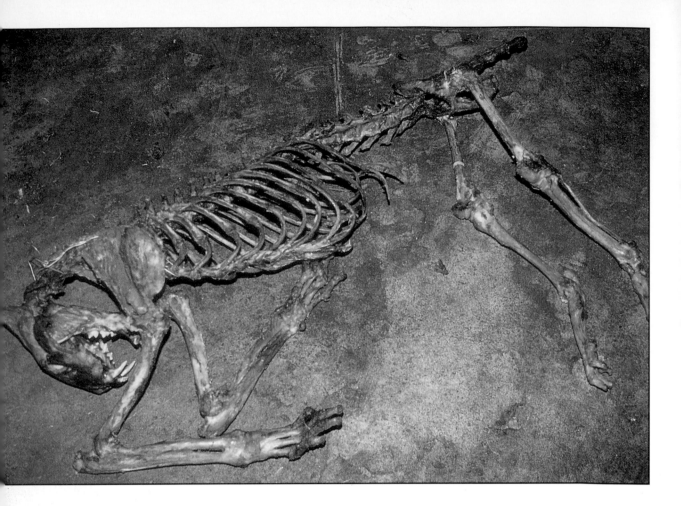

# Tigers and Man

People have been hunting tigers for a long time. For more than 1000 years, people have been killing tigers so that they can use their body parts in Asian medicines. Almost all parts of a tiger can be used, but the most important of all is tiger bone. This may be made into a number of products, including pills and medicinal wine and soup.

In the early days, the hunters had only spears and bows and arrows, and tigers were often able to escape. But when

*A tiger skeleton on sale in China. People pay as much as $400 a pound for tiger bone.*

guns were invented, tigers became much easier to kill – not only for local hunters but for other people, too. Visitors from all over the world began to travel to Asia just to hunt tigers for sport. Many thousands of tigers were killed in this way. The invention of the gun also meant that people could kill animals for food more easily. A number of the animals people eat, such as deer, are also hunted by tigers. People killed so many of these that tigers began to struggle to find their prey.

*Once, people traveled on elephants to hunt the tiger. Now the passengers are tourists, hoping for a glimpse of this beautiful cat.*

## Tigers and Man

A far greater problem was that people also began destroying the tigers' forest and grassland homes. They did this because the human population was increasing fast. More and more land was needed for building villages, planting crops, and grazing farm animals. People began to cut down the forests and plow up the grasslands.

The more people moved into tigers' territories, the more tigers and people came into contact. As people continued to kill or push out the tiger's natural prey, hungry tigers turned on farmers' livestock to satisfy their appetites. They also attacked people.

*A tiger bursts from cover to attack its prey. Tigers have a bad reputation for attacking people. In fact, few tigers become man-eaters.*

It is not clear what makes a tiger become a "man-eater." One suggestion is that a tiger may attack a person if it feels in danger of being attacked itself. Another suggestion is that attacks on people occur if a tiger is sick and weak and too slow to catch its normal prey. It is also possible that a tiger will turn to man-eating for the same reason as it turns to eating livestock – if it cannot find enough of its natural prey to feed on. Whatever the reason, people became terrified of tigers. They would not take the risk of having tigers living close by and killed them whenever they could.

*A magnificent Indochinese tiger patrols its territory. Besides being hunted for their body parts, tigers are killed for their beautiful striped coats.*

# Saving the Tiger

With all these problems to face, it is not surprising that the tiger became endangered. In 1969, **conservationists** reported that tigers were in serious danger throughout their range. The number of tigers left in the wild had dropped from over 100,000 to only 5000. Something had to be done quickly to save these beautiful cats.

In 1972, leading conservation organizations set up "Operation Tiger." This included a huge poster campaign to show people just how few tigers were left and to persuade them to give money to help save the tiger from extinction.

*Ranthambhore Tiger Reserve in India is a protected area set up by Project Tiger. The building in the picture used to be a palace.*

The money collected was then used to pay for a tiger-protection program in India called "Project Tiger."

This program set up nine protected areas of land called **reserves** In these protected areas, the tigers' habitat was to be carefully looked after, and the animals themselves were to be safe from hunters. Some of the money was used to pay local people to stop **poaching** (illegal hunting).

Project Tiger has been successful. In India alone, the number of wild tigers is said to have risen from 1827 to 3000 during the 1970s, and to 4000 by 1983. Today there are 18 tiger reserves in India and further reserves in other Asian countries. There are now twice as many tigers living in reserves as there were 20 years ago.

*A tiger is filmed as it strolls down a track in the Sariska Tiger Reserve in India.*

*Many tigers are kept in zoos around the world. This male Indian tiger, pictured here with his keeper, was raised by people at a zoo in Kent, England.*

Project Tiger has helped save the tiger for now, but the cat remains in danger. The human population of Asia continues to grow, and people are still clearing land. Soon the only tiger habitat left will be in the reserves. These areas can hold only a limited number of tigers. Also, hunting tigers for use in medicine – although it is illegal – still goes on, even in reserves, and in spite of government penalties against poachers.

Unless further action is taken immediately, the tiger may yet disappear forever in the wild. A way needs to be found of managing what tiger habitat is left so that both the cats and people can benefit. But most importantly, the poaching needs to be stopped, or Project Tiger's work will have been for nothing. In 1994, the Global Tiger Forum was set up to to try to bring the trade in tiger parts to an end. If this organization succeeds, the tiger may still be prowling the forests and grasslands of Asia in years to come.

*The tiger can still be saved, but only if the hunting stops now.*

# Useful Addresses

For more information about tigers and how you can help protect them, contact these organizations:

**Conservation International**
1015 18th Street NW
Suite 1000
Washington, D.C. 20036

**National Wildlife Federation**
1400 16th Street NW
Washington, D.C. 20036

**New York Zoological Society/The Wildlife Conservation Society**
18th Street and Southern Boulevard
Bronx, New York 10460

**U.S. Fish and Wildlife Service**
Endangered Species and Habitat
Conservation
400 Arlington Square
18th and C Streets NW
Washington, D.C. 20240

**World Wildlife Fund**
1250 24th Street NW
Washington, D.C. 20037

**World Wildlife Fund Canada**
90 Eglinton Avenue East
Suite 504
Toronto
Ontario M4P 2Z7

# Further Reading

*Close to the Wild: Siberian Tigers in a Zoo* Thomas Cajacob and Theresa Burdon (Minneapolis: Lerner, 1986)

*Endangered Species* National Wildlife Federation Staff (Vienna, VA: National Wildlife Federation, 1991)

*Endangered Wildlife of the World* (New York: Marshall Cavendish Corporation, 1993)

*Jane Goodall's Animal World: Tigers* Ruth Ashby (New York: Atheneum, 1990)

*Lions and Tigers and Leopards: The Big Cats* Jennifer C. Urquhart (Washington, D.C.: National Geographic Society, 1990)

*Wildlife of the World* (New York: Marshall Cavendish Corporation, 1994)

# Glossary

**Adapt**: To change in order to survive in new conditions.

**Canine teeth**: The four large, pointed teeth found at the front corners of a carnivore's mouth. There are two in the upper jaw and two in the lower.

**Captivity**: Confinement; for animals, usually in a cage.

**Carnivore**: An animal that eats meat.

**Conservationist** (Kon-ser-VAY-shun-ist): A person who protects and preserves the Earth's natural resources, such as animals, plants, and soil.

**Den**: A hole or cave that an animal uses as its home.

**Extinct** (Ex-TINKT): No longer living anywhere in the world.

**Habitat**: The place where an animal lives. For example, the tiger's habitat is grassland or the forest.

**Mammal**: A kind of animal that is warm-blooded and has a backbone. Most mammals are covered with fur or have hair. Females have glands that produce milk to feed their young.

**Mate**: When a male and female get together to produce young.

**Poaching**: Illegal hunting.

**Prey**: An animal that is hunted and eaten by another animal.

**Rainforest**: A forest that has heavy rainfall much of the year.

**Range**. The area in the world in which a particular kind of animal can be found.

**Reserve**: Land that has been set aside for plants and animals to live in without being harmed.

**Territory**: The piece of land in which an animal lives. Some animals, such as tigers, defend their territory against others of their own kind.

**Tropical**: Having to do with or found in the tropics, the warm region of the Earth near the Equator. For example, a tropical rainforest.

# Index